Scavengers:
Eating Nature's Trash

Coyotes

Emma Carlson Berne

PowerKiDS press™

New York

Published in 2015 by The Rosen Publishing Group, Inc.
29 East 21st Street, New York, NY 10010

First Edition

Editor: Joanne Randolph
Book Design: Joe Carney
Photo Research: Katie Stryker

Photo Credits: Cover, p. 19 Yair Leibovich/Shutterstock.com; pp. 5, 21 Fuse/Thinkstock; p. 6 Brent Paull/iStock/Thinkstock; p. 9 kojihirano/Shutterstock.com; p. 10 Songbird839/iStock/Thinkstock; p. 11 MountainHardcore/Shutterstock.com; p. 12 Tom Lynn/Getty Images; p. 13 Jim Gensheimer/America 24-7/Getty Images; p. 14 TOM MCHUGH/Photo Researchers/Getty Images; p. 15 Doug Steakley/Lonely Planet Images/Getty Images; p. 16 Comstock/Stockbyte/Thinkstock; p. 17 Tom Brakefield/Stockbyte/Thinkstock; p. 18 John E Marriott/All Canada Photos/Getty Images; p. 20 Critterbiz/Shutterstock; p. 22 FredS/Shutterstock.com.

Library of Congress Cataloging-in-Publication Data

Berne, Emma Carlson, author.
  Coyotes / by Emma Carlson Berne. — First edition.
      pages cm. — (Scavengers: eating nature's trash)
  Includes index.
  ISBN 978-1-4777-6607-1 (library binding) — ISBN 978-1-4777-6608-8 (pbk.) — ISBN 978-1-4777-6609-5 (6-pack)
  1. Coyote—Juvenile literature. 2. Scavengers (Zoology)—Juvenile literature. 3. Ecology—Juvenile literature. I. Title.
  QL737.C22B476 2015
  599.773—dc23
                        2013051025

Manufactured in the United States of America

CPSIA Compliance Information: Batch #WS14PK6: For Further Information contact Rosen Publishing, New York, New York at 1-800-237-9932

Contents

Cool Coyotes

Many animals in America are losing the battle against **habitat** loss. People have taken over more and more land. Animals such as cougars, wolves, and bears have become fewer in number since they have less space in which to live.

Some animals seem to be thriving, though, despite the increase in people. For example, the number of coyotes has gone up. Partly, this is because coyotes are **adaptable** hunters, **scavengers**, and **foragers**. They can hunt alone, in pairs, or in packs. They can eat live or dead animals, fruits, and food scraps. Do you want to find out more about these adaptable animals?

Coyotes are at home in many different places. They can live in the wilderness, in backyards, and even in big cities.

Where Are the Coyotes?

Coyotes will travel up to 25 miles (40 km) from their **dens** to hunt. They can travel up to 400 miles (644 km) if they need to find new **territory**.

Coyotes are not bothered by the snow and are good at hunting for animals burrowing beneath the surface.

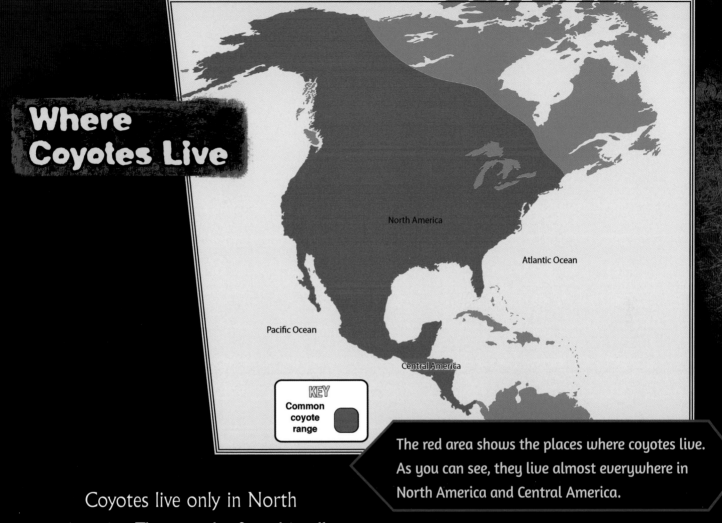

North America

Atlantic Ocean

Pacific Ocean

Central America

KEY
Common coyote range

The red area shows the places where coyotes live. As you can see, they live almost everywhere in North America and Central America.

Coyotes live only in North America. They can be found in all 50 states, Mexico, and most of Canada, even the very cold Far North. There are 19 **subspecies** of coyotes. Coyotes living in northern areas are usually larger, while those in the South are smaller. Different subspecies might have heads that are shaped a little differently. Some have fur that is almost black, while others have fur that is very light tan and white. Some subspecies in the South and Mexico might have very short fur. In the North, coyotes are more likely to have longer, warmer fur.

Coyotes Can Live Anywhere

Coyotes can make their homes in the desert, in the mountains, on the prairies, in the suburbs, in farmland, and even in cities. They can live almost anywhere they can find food. Luckily for coyotes, almost any kind of animal or **carrion** can be food.

When they can, coyotes prefer to live near some sort of water, like a river or creek, and near tall grass and shrubs. These plants shelter lots of rodents, which coyotes hunt and eat.

Swimming Coyotes

Coyotes are good swimmers. They have even been found on islands. **Biologists** believe the coyotes swam to the islands from the mainland.

This coyote trots through the desert in New Mexico. Coyotes are able to adapt to many different living conditions. They will eat whatever food is available.

Social Structure

Wolves, which are related to coyotes, hunt in packs. Coyotes sometimes hunt in small packs, too, when they are after larger **prey**. Usually, coyotes hunt either alone or in pairs. In pairs, they use the buddy system. One coyote might distract the prey while the other one pounces.

Coyotes are often seen alone. They hunt for small prey on their own so they do not have to share with another coyote.

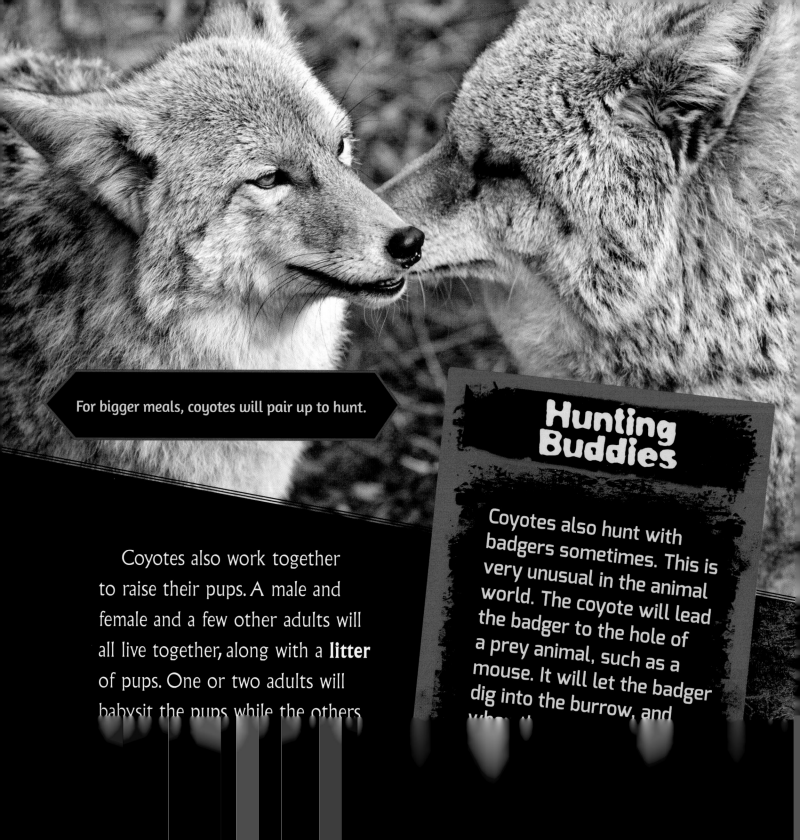

For bigger meals, coyotes will pair up to hunt.

Hunting Buddies

Coyotes also hunt with badgers sometimes. This is very unusual in the animal world. The coyote will lead the badger to the hole of a prey animal, such as a mouse. It will let the badger dig into the burrow, and when the

Coyotes also work together to raise their pups. A male and female and a few other adults will all live together, along with a **litter** of pups. One or two adults will babysit the pups while the others

Key to Success

People have gradually taken over the natural homes of **predators** like wolves and cougars. These animals have slowly been reduced in number. Coyotes have not, though. In fact, there are now more coyotes than ever. Coyotes now live in states they never lived in before.

This coyote makes its home in the city of Milwaukee, in Wisconsin.

Living near people gives coyotes access to animals killed by cars, as well as garbage and food scraps discarded by people.

This is because coyotes can eat almost anything and live almost anywhere. They can hunt at night or in the day. They can eat wild live animals or discarded human food, roadkill, or other dead animals. They know how to avoid people and traps that might hurt them. They can live in the cold, in the heat, or in rocky or sandy areas. The coyote's ability to adapt has been the key to its success.

What Does the Coyote Say?

Coyotes use their big ears, as well as their teeth, tails, and bodies to **communicate** with each other. Many signals are sent using body language. For example, when two coyotes are face to face, one might roll over on its back, exposing its belly and throat. It is saying, "You're in charge" to the other coyote. One coyote might show its teeth, stiffen its back, and raise the hair on its neck while growling. This means, "Watch out! I might attack you."

Coyotes howl together at sunrise and sunset, when communicating over a long distance, or when trying to find other coyotes.

Here two coyotes are greeting each other for the first time. Ears that are slightly back signal that the coyote plans to be friendly. If they were flat back against the head, it would mean this coyote is frightened.

Coyotes communicate with their voices, too. They howl, bark, or growl to call other coyotes, when playing, or to let another coyote know they do not like something.

Great Hunters

If a coyote spots prey it wants to catch, it may sink down low on its legs and move very slowly forward until it can get close enough to surprise the animal. This is called stalking.

A coyote will try to catch and eat most animals it comes across. This one chases down a raccoon.

Coyotes are excellent hunters. They use their keen senses of hearing, smell, and sight to help them.

A coyote might be hunting a mouse in tall grass. It uses its sense of smell to find it and will also listen for mouse-like rustles in the grass. When it hears one, the coyote freezes and creeps up on its prey. Then it leaps suddenly from its back feet, pouncing on the mouse with its front feet. It swallows the mouse in one or two bites.

Coyotes are too small to kill big prey like healthy elk or deer on their own. They will work in groups to take down this larger prey.

Coyotes Are Scavengers, Too

Coyotes are good hunters, but they are also great scavengers. They will raid fields and orchards to get at fruit. Sometimes, they irritate farmers by taking one bite of a piece of fruit and leaving the rest. They seem to like melon best of all.

Meat for a coyote does not have to be fresh. This coyote is chewing on the dead body of a moose that looks like it has been there for a while.

Animals that will eat whatever presents itself, including old, rotting animals, are called opportunistic feeders.

Coyotes will clean up dead deer and elk killed by cars or hunters. They will kill sick or old animals. This is all part of their job as nature's janitors.

A Tough Stomach

Coyotes can digest just about anything. Chunks of tire, leather, and harness buckles have all been found in coyotes' stomachs.

Life as a Baby Coyote

Like many mammals, coyotes work together to raise their young, which are called pups. The mother usually digs a den underground. The mother will move the pups to a different den if she feels they are in danger.

Two coyote pups peek out of their den. They might be waiting for a parent to return with lunch.

Coyote pups copy their mothers to learn how to behave.

The pups come out of the den after about two weeks. They are ready to explore their world. Their mother eats meat and vomits it up. The pups eat this soft, digested meat, just as human babies eat baby food. The pups play fight and pretend to hunt. Soon they go along on family hunts, observing what the adults do and learning to hunt for themselves.

Living with Coyotes

Over time, people have trapped, killed, and poisoned coyotes. Coyotes stay out of the way of people, though, and are not aggressive. They eat the mice and rats that can harm farmers' crops. They clean up dead and sick animals that can spread disease to humans and pets.

If you ever see one of these beautiful predators in your neighborhood, take a moment to stop and admire it. Then thank the coyote for being a helpful part of our natural world.

As coyotes live closer to people, it is important that people respect them. If you see a coyote, do not try to get close to it. Observe the animal in its natural habitat and leave it alone.

Do not feed the coyotes.

Glossary

adaptable (uh-DAP-tuh-bul) Able to change to fit new conditions.

biologists (by-AH-luh-jists) Scientists who study plants and animals.

carrion (KAR-ee-un) Dead, rotting flesh.

communicate (kuh-MYOO-nih-kayt) To share facts or feelings.

dens (DENZ) Wild animals' homes.

foragers (FOR-ij-erz) Animals that hunt or search for food.

habitat (HA-buh-tat) The surroundings where an animal or a plant naturally lives.

litter (LIH-ter) A group of baby animals all born at the same time from the same mother.

predators (PREH-duh-terz) Animals that kill other animals for food.

prey (PRAY) An animal that is hunted by another animal for food.

scavengers (SKA-ven-jurz) Animals that eat dead things.

subspecies (SUB-spee-sheez) Animals in the same species, or group, that look slightly different and live in different places.

territory (TER-uh-tor-ee) Land or space that animals guard for their use.

Index

Websites

Due to the changing nature of Internet links, PowerKids Press has developed an online list of websites related to the subject of this book. This site is updated regularly. Please use this link to access the list: www.powerkidslinks.com/scav/coyo/